Developing Successful Retail in Underserved Urban Markets

Developing Successful Retail in Underserved Urban Markets

INTERNATIONAL COUNCIL OF SHOPPING CENTERS
NEW YORK

In cooperation with Business for Social Responsibility (BSR)

This publication is designed to provide accurate and authoritative information in regard to the subject matter covered. It is sold with the understanding that the publisher is not engaged in rendering legal, accounting, or other professional services. If legal advice or other expert assistance is required, the services of a competent professional person should be sought.

> —*From a Declaration of Principles jointly adopted by a Committee of the American Bar Association and a Committee of Publishers.*

Companies, professional groups, clubs and other organizations may qualify for special terms when ordering quantities of more than 20 of this title.

Published by
INTERNATIONAL COUNCIL OF SHOPPING CENTERS
Publications Department
1221 Avenue of the Americas
New York, NY 10020-1099

BOOK DESIGN: SD Designs
COVER DESIGN: DK&G Creative Services
Cover photographs of Penn Mar Shopping Center, Forestville, Maryland, courtesy of The Rappaport Companies

ICSC Catalog Number: 239

International Standard Book Number: 1-58268-039-6

Printed in the United States of America

CONTENTS

ABOUT THE INTERNATIONAL COUNCIL OF SHOPPING CENTERS AND BUSINESS FOR SOCIAL RESPONSIBILITY

INTERNATIONAL COUNCIL OF SHOPPING CENTERS

The International Council of Shopping Centers (ICSC) is the trade association for retail real estate. Founded in 1957, its now more than 44,000 members in the U.S., Canada, and more than 75 other countries include owners, developers, retailers, lenders, and other professionals as well as academics and public officials. ICSC's Alliance Program is an effort dedicated to fostering relationships and strategic alliances between the public and private sector. These critical partnerships assure that growth and prosperity are sustained in our communities. In this effort, local and regional meetings and deal-making sessions serve as the forum to introduce the intricacies of the shopping center industry to representatives of state and local governments and community-based organizations. In addition, these forums provide the public sector with the opportunity to share the complexities and issues that face local communities today.

BUSINESS FOR SOCIAL RESPONSIBILITY

Since 1992, Business for Social Responsibility (BSR) has helped companies of all sizes and sectors to achieve business objectives and efficiencies in ways that demonstrate respect for ethical values, people, communities, and the environment. A leading global business partner, BSR equips its member companies with the expertise to design, implement and evaluate successful, socially responsible business policies, practices and processes. BSR provides tools, training, advisory services and collaborative opportunities in person, in print and online that equip companies to implement socially responsible business practices that serve business goals. Today, more than 1,400 member and affiliated companies worldwide participate in BSR's global network of programs and partnerships.

INTRODUCTION

Lack of retailers is a critical issue for many communities across the nation, particularly in inner cities. At least three major studies in the last few years concluded that urban markets remain underserved because retailers misunderstand the potential of these markets. The **International Council of Shopping Centers** (ICSC) and **Business for Social Responsibility** (BSR) both began independently looking at the issue in the late 1990s. ICSC through its Alliance Program tried to respond to comments from local governments such as "why are we having so much trouble getting retailers to come to our community?" BSR began an initiative in 1999 as a response to retailers who wanted to access the untapped opportunities in America's underserved urban markets. Both ICSC and BSR learned from all of the parties involved in retail development that while a lack of accurate market information was an important problem, the explanation of why inner-city locations are underserved goes far beyond that single issue. For example, BSR learned, among other things, that retailers often face significant challenges working with local governments in the siting and development process.

The two organizations developed a unique partnership to stimulate a dialogue between all retail development process participants and to address the challenges and obstacles more comprehensively, ultimately facilitating development in underserved markets.

It was against this backdrop that ICSC and BSR undertook the first step in an effort to stimulate dialogue—a survey to determine the primary challenges retailers face when locating in underserved urban markets and what changes or incentives would facilitate the development process. This publication examines the results of this survey and is based on a report entitled *Development in Underserved Retail Markets*, which was jointly produced by ICSC and BSR (and co-written by Cynthia Stewart, Director, Local Government Relations, ICSC and Alexis Morris, Manager, Community Investment, BSR). For the purpose of the survey, these retail markets were defined as low-income urban communities that have inadequate access to products and services.

The survey found that eleven factors are regarded by more than 80% of the respondents as significant obstacles to entry into underserved markets (i.e., factors rated "very significant" or "somewhat significant"). These factors are, in descending order of importance:

1. Crime/perceived crime
2. Insufficient concentration of the retailer's target customer
3. Lack of consumer purchasing power for the retailer's product
4. Potential shrinkage
5. Rent
6. Buildout/rehabilitation costs
7. Site identification
8. Inadequate parking
9. Higher operating costs
10. Construction and development costs
11. Lack of amenities to attract out-of-neighborhood employees

A copy of the survey results is included in the Appendix.

The results of the underserved markets survey clearly indicate that there is a far broader range of issues than just consumer spending power that determine whether retailers locate stores in underserved markets. Post-survey, ICSC and BSR members recognized that it was not enough to simply identify the issues and concerns that inhibit development in underserved urban markets—that as an industry it would be better to take a more proactive, definitive approach to address the issues.

In this spirit, the survey results were used to stimulate a broader conversation about what can be done to address the challenges and barriers identified. A select group of public officials, developers, brokers and retailers was convened to discuss these survey results in depth, and compile tangible recommendations to address the concerns.

This publication is not meant to simplify the issue or lay blame with any one stakeholder or interest group. It is hoped that the survey and recommendations developed at the forum, along with new illustrative case examples, will provoke thought and stimulate dialogue as well as serve as a catalyst in the formation of new partnerships and relationships, information sharing, and educational sessions. The end goal is to help promote retail development in underserved markets.

CHALLENGES AND RECOMMENDATIONS

Development is a complicated process and retailers alone are not responsible for markets remaining underserved. While there are many important parties involved in the development process, such as brokers and financial intermediaries, there are four critical interest groups that can work individually and in partnership to overcome the challenges and obstacles to development in underserved markets. The four key interest groups are:

- Community (residents, community-based organizations)
- Developers
- Government (elected officials and professional staff)
- Retailers

All affected parties must implement a comprehensive plan to ensure the effective execution of a positive, safe, and successful entry into underserved markets.

Ultimately, it is retailers in partnership with developers that drive development. Therefore, it is important for the public officials and community leaders to understand the "cycle" of economic development in general and the retail development process specifically in order to have realistic expectations for development and to work productively with developers to meet the development objectives of the community. For example, even if all the identified challenges and issues are addressed, in most cases there will still be a necessary progression to the retail development of underserved markets—often beginning with fast food restaurants and drugstores, progressing to grocery stores and discount apparel and shoes and eventually ending with specialty retailers and higher-priced concepts.

In general, the following are key points that affect retail development in underserved markets:

- Crime is a significant issue. However, in some cases, it is the perception of crime, rather than actual crime statistics, that influences development decisions.

- It is important for retailers and developers to develop good early working relationships with the community and public safety officials.
- With increasing diversity across America, there is a consensus that many retailers' traditional target customer profile may not represent the more diverse marketplace of today and the future.
- Traditional market data and analysis may be inaccurate or misrepresent the economic potential and purchasing power of underserved markets.
- Many municipalities would benefit from more targeted marketing and communications strategies.
- It can take longer and may be more complicated to develop in an urban area, which translates to higher costs. Reducing the cost and time it takes to develop can help promote more development in underserved markets.
- Cost of site preparedness and rehabilitation can be more expensive in these markets.
- While urban markets are generally more pedestrian-friendly, the reality is that people still need cars/parking or access to transportation.
- Operating costs are often higher in urban, underserved markets, but this can be offset by the higher sales potential of these markets.
- Accessibility to public transportation and improved safety and security can help recruit and retain employees.
- Government tax incentive programs can assist in reduction of operating costs.

This publication is divided into four major areas: 1) Public Safety; 2) Market Identification and Site Selection Issues; 3) Development and Construction Issues; and 4) Retailers' Operational Issues. Each section highlights suggestions or steps the four interest groups (communities, local governments, developers, retailers) can use to address the issues, help promote a better climate for development, and bring needed services to underserved communities. Illustrative case profiles and examples of successful programs and projects appear throughout to provide further insight.

Crime and perceived crime are very high on the list of challenges and/or concerns facing retailers and developers when considering entry into underserved markets. Often it is past history and/or the perception of crime rather than actual current crime statistics that motivate or influence development decisions. Local governments and community groups could benefit from facing this issue head-on in their efforts to attract retailers and developers to create new businesses within their specific market area.

This issue is best addressed when local governments and community groups work in concert with each other. A suggestion is the formulation of a strategic approach, perhaps through the development of a prepackaged crime initiative. This program could be designed to address both the developer and retailer concerns for safety of their employees, potential customers, and community residents.

Section Highlights:

- Crime is a significant issue. However, in some cases, it is the perception of crime, rather than actual crime statistics, that influences development decisions.
- It is important for retailers and developers to develop good early working relationships with the community and public safety officials.

In addition, retailers and developers should accept some measure of responsibility for developing good early working relationships with community (neighborhood groups, community leadership) and public safety officials (local government).

Suggestions to Four Critical Interest Groups

Community

- **Partner with local government to develop strategies to address crime issues**—Community groups can work with local police to develop safety, security, and prevention strategies that benefit local residents as well as businesses. Individuals in the community can also become involved in crime prevention programs such as Neighborhood Watch. Support the local government with their marketing initiatives and efforts to overcome perceptions of crime.
- **Involve police and police leadership in developing patrol patterns based on store openings and operating hours.** New stores can be "challenged" by security issues in the beginning. Local police may need to have a stronger presence in the very beginning.
- **Encourage support for new retail ventures in the community.**

Walgreens opened this store—its 3,000th—in Chicago's Greektown neighborhood in May 2000. One of the most visible Walgreens in the city, the 24-hour store sits in the shadow of the Sears Tower just west of the Loop. Every day, it is visible to 150,000 passing motorists on the Dan Ryan Expressway. Walgreens worked closely with city planning officials to design a building that would marry Mayor Daley's desire for a store fronting the street with the convenient, well-lit, safe parking Walgreens' customers demand. The result is a store fronting Halsted Street on one side, but with a parking lot on the corner. To further respect the neighborhood, Walgreens included Greek lettering on the building, Greek columns on the parking lot corner and an all-brick, two-story facade that fits the historical feel of Halsted Street. The store was well received by city officials and customers from the day its doors opened and has become one of the city's busiest Walgreens.

Government

- **Careful evaluation of crime statistics**—Local governments should carefully evaluate crime statistic reports on a community or market basis. When statistics do not support public perception, the local government could proactively present that data to potential developers or retailers. When statistics indicate potential problems with crime in underserved markets, then governments should work to develop initiatives and strategies to reduce crime in those areas and market those initiatives or efforts to potential developers and retailers.

- **Develop proactive prevention strategies**—Local governments should identify potential development locations and prepare a strategy to address crime and safety concerns up front before development is begun.

- **Develop marketing and communication strategies to address perceptions of crime**—Out-of-town brokers or developers may be unfamiliar with a community, and their decisions may be influenced by past negative media reports about a neighborhood. Local governments can actively market their communities, challenge media on fairness in reporting and encourage media to highlight the positive attributes of urban communities, rather than continuing to focus on past historical crime reporting.

- **Focus on public access to sites**—Cities can work with local community and transportation planners to create effective public transportation routes and transfer stations that increase safety and reduce the potential for crime.

- **Collaborate with local police and police leadership**—Police need to be more responsive to retail requests. Cities could facilitate the placement of police substations in shopping centers and establish or modify existing patrol patterns.

- **Evaluate the impact of design requirements upon safety**—Cities may need to adjust lighting, design and accessibility requirements in ways that support safety. For example, parking may need to be convenient to the front door as opposed to often more desirable remote parking or rear parking.

Developers

- **Modify parking**—In areas where there is a perception of high crime, developers may need to create parking that is convenient to the front door, as opposed to removed parking. They also need to provide visible, well-lit parking lots.

- **Consider installing appropriate fencing**—Developers may want to consider installing fencing as a strategy to promote safety and security. For example, some developers have found fencing in front of the stores to be a successful deterrent, while others have installed fencing along the entire perimeter. However, it is important to be aware that fencing can be a sensitive issue in many communities, and developers who want to create successful shopping centers need to be sensitive to the community's viewpoint.

- **Incorporate security considerations into facility design**—Developers need to create visibility and develop structures that protect storefronts. They should install high-intensity lighting in the front and back of the shopping center store.

- **Establish early relationships with law enforcement**—Developers need to establish community and local law enforcement relationships as soon as a site is identified or construction is started, well before any stores are open.
- **Provide financial assistance to retailers**—Developers may need to make allowances in common area maintenance (CAM) costs for retailers to offset security costs and create a visible security presence.

Retailers

- **Create a close working partnership with community and police to address all community concerns that effect store presence**—Retailers also need to develop early relationships (before store opening) with local police departments and formulate joint partnerships with police and community leaders to address issues that might lead to potential crime.
- **Share success stories**—Retailers need to be willing to share successful strategies that will help other companies learn how to enter and operate in underserved markets successfully.
- **Adapt security strategies for urban markets**—Retailers should hire and train members of management from the local community to complement existing management staff. They should develop a management-training program that emphasizes a personalized, hands-on approach of doing business in urban markets. Retailers may need to make modifications that include design, security training, management selection (do managers represent the community) and hiring practices (from within the community) to facilitate success in these markets. Internal loss prevention programs must be non-threatening and include increased internal security, increased security training, and customer interaction.

Incorporating Security Into Facility Design

CITY HEIGHTS RETAIL VILLAGE

San Diego, the City Heights Retail Village, a 110,000-sq.-ft. neighborhood shopping center anchored by an Albertsons supermarket, was developed as the last phase of a master redevelopment plan spearheaded by the city. The first component of that plan was the development of a police substation one block away from the shopping center site. The shopping center project was developed by a joint venture comprised of CityLink Investment Corp. and The Retail Initiative, Inc. The Mid-City Police Sub-Station and Community Gymnasium opened in 1996 and reportedly helped reduce the crime rate in the City Heights neigborhood by 39% in the 4 years subsequent to its opening. It was the first component of a master redevelopment plan that included a new public library, an elementary school, a community college, and the shopping center. The substation includes a high-ceiling gym and 2,850-sq.-ft. second story that is used as a meeting place for community activities. The substation is not part of the shopping center site, but is across the street within the immediate vicinity.

WESTLAND PLAZA

Westland Plaza in Jackson, Mississippi, was the state's first modern-style shopping center. However, by the early 1990s time and changes in area demographics led to a significant decline of the center. According to Harold Lathon, Director of Economic Development for the City of Jackson at the time, "The center had deteriorated to the point where it was not only unsightly but crime was making it a real problem." Westland Plaza Associates acquired the center in 1986. In 1996, they brought in Stirling Properties to take over the leasing and management with a mandate to enhance value for the owners and restore Westland Plaza as a neighborhood center. Stirling took measures to counteract possible crime and vandalism by requesting a police presence in the center. As a result, a 2,500-square-foot Neighborhood Enforcement Team (NET) facility, staffed by the Jackson Police Department, was opened. In addition to the NET facility, Stirling Properties performed a complete overhaul of the shopping center, including a new parking lot, high-powered parking lot lights to assist in the deterrence of crime and to promote safety, new facades, and new pylons. There has been a significant drop in reported crime from 1999 to 2002. During the redevelopment, the center retained all existing tenants, renewing and renegotiating their leases and having them revamp their tenant spaces and signage. Improvements at Westland Plaza have significantly strengthened the center with 84% of retail space leased by the end of 2000 and tenants reporting increased sales and increased foot traffic. This center has once again become the definition of a neighborhood center with a food store, post office, and the daily neighborhood conveniences along with about 28 soft good apparel-related stores.

Westland Plaza Before

Westland Plaza After

Many retailers believe that underserved markets do not have enough of their target customers or have enough purchasing power—the consensus being that retailers and developers need to look at different models and types of market data that more accurately capture the potential of urban, underserved markets. Participants acknowledged that a lack of solid market data has been a barrier for many corporations entering these markets. Traditional market analysis (e.g., using indicators such as household income to project sales) has been proven inadequate. For example, reported income is often underestimated for low-income people, as it does not factor in the cash economy, which is a significant and growing source of income. New and innovative market indicators (concentrated buying power, spending patterns) combined with information from other businesses operating in these communities can provide a more accurate picture of the potential opportunities. The charts on the following two pages illustrate such innovative indicators.

In addition to identifying customers and measuring purchasing power, identifying and locating adequate sites presents a significant challenge due to lack of experience in urban markets, fewer location options, and smaller parcel sizes.

Section Highlights:

- With increasing diversity across America, there is a consensus that many retailers' traditional target customer profile may not represent the more diverse marketplace of today and the future.

- Traditional market data and analysis may not adequately measure the economic potential and purchasing power of underserved markets.

- Many municipalities would benefit from more targeted marketing and communications strategies.

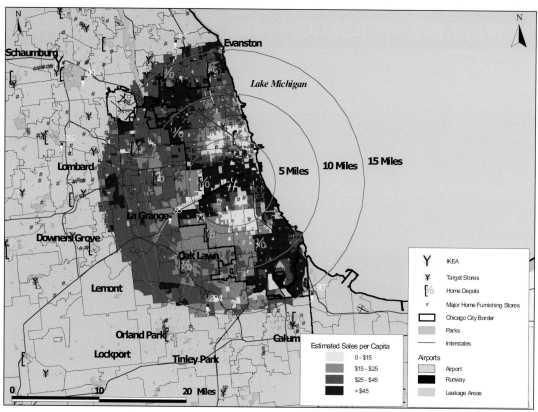

A thorough market study that estimates sales per capita and retail competition is necessary to attract national retailers, such as this study of the Chicago urban area. (Provided by MetroEdge.)

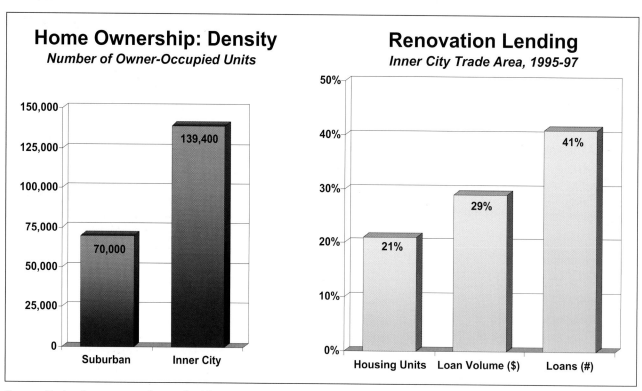

Inner-city trade areas can have significant home ownership activity. Looking at renovation activity can also be important for understanding the purchasing power related to home improvement, furnishings and other household items. (Provided by MetroEdge.)

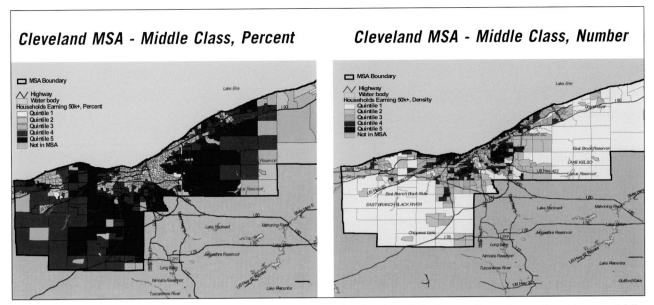

Counting the number of middle-class households captures the density of the inner city and reveals a strong middle class. (Provided by MetroEdge.)

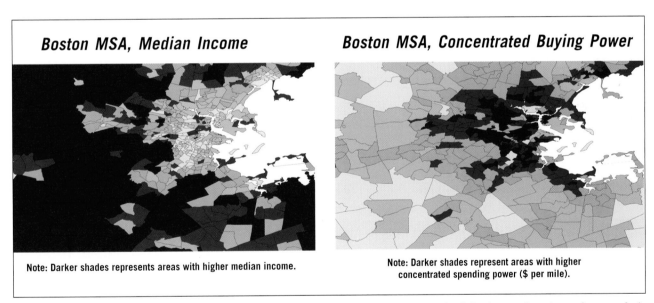

Conventional methods of market analysis tend to underestimate the potential of the inner city. A good example is the common focus on median income as an indicator of buying power. Despite a lower median income, the inner city has significant buying power. (Provided by MetroEdge.)

Suggestions to Four Critical Interest Groups

Forum participants had the following suggestions for ways the four interest groups can address market identification and site selection challenges in underserved markets:

Community

- **Help with market preparation**—The community can work to improve the visual standards, presentation and quality of local businesses and retailers. In addition, local community development corporations (CDCs) and faith-based organizations can be valuable partners in site preparation and development.

Government

- **Provide quality data on the potential of the market**—Cities need to be aware that traditional demographic data is not always accurate and timely and needs to be supplemented and enhanced to reflect the true makeup of a community and available customer base, such as different spending habits and buying patterns. Many local governments can take a more proactive approach to improve the marketing of their constituencies to potential retailers and developers. This includes providing better and more customized data on high-potential local markets, focusing on site opportunities in the market area and community buying potential.
- **Identify sites ready for development**—Local governments can highlight sites to retailers and developers and assemble land necessary for development.
- **Create foot traffic**—To create traffic in these markets and increase the potential customer base, government and developers can collaborate to locate services such as bill-paying centers featuring utility companies, the department of motor vehicles, cable companies, postal services, etc. However, communities should designate sites for government use that are adjacent or near to sites for retail development, not on the best sites for retail development.
- **Market and communicate local opportunities**—There are many steps cities can take to market and communicate development opportunities. They can facilitate or conduct tours of urban markets, or collaborate with local real estate professionals to bring retailers and developers to available sites. Websites are an increasingly important means of communication for marketing inner-city retail sites. Creating comprehensive marketing strategies can also help make urban neighborhoods more competitive.
- **Help develop and recruit franchisees**—Cities should develop programs that can help retailers identify potential local franchisees and facilitate access to capital and technical assistance for franchisees. In addition, cities may need to think of more aggressive tactics such as absorbing and reformatting retail concepts that have become outdated (e.g., lot depths may need to be redesigned and deepened in many traditional business corridors). This will need to be preceded by aggressive development/business planning.

Before

Sometimes the best redevelopment opportunities exist in an old seemingly dying center, as is the case here with Penn Mar Shopping Center in Forestville, Maryland, redeveloped by The Rappaport Companies.

After

Developers

- **Don't oversimplify markets**—Part of the challenge of developing in underserved markets is that they are not homogeneous communities that lend themselves to "cookie-cutter" type developments. There is a greater need to consider natural physical barriers to neighborhoods (interstates, public transportation), as well as local traffic patterns, when conducting market analysis.
- **Customize market analysis**—Data analysis has to incorporate the most current and available statistical data. Developers may need more sophisticated market analysis that captures the potential of underserved markets such as different spending habits and buying patterns.

2000 census data suggests the positive trends are emerging in America's cities:

- As a group, the largest cities grew faster in the 1990s than in the 1980s
- CBDs increased in population during the 1990s

"Understanding the Retail Business Potential of Inner Cities," *Journal of Economic Issues,* December 2003 (Vol. XXXVII, No. 4), pp. 1075-1105 written by Weiler, Stephan, Jesse Silverstein, Kace Chalmers, Erin Lavey, William Rogers and Benjamin Widner.

Article Highlights: These researchers picked up from where the 1999 HUD study, *New Markets: The Untapped Retail Buying Power In America's Inner Cities,* left off. That HUD study found that "inner-city neighborhoods possess enormous retail purchasing power," but those markets are often significantly under-stored. This study raises the question: **how should potential spending power of inner cities be measured?** The authors argue that inner-city household buying power should not be measured on a household-income basis, as is usually done, but on a **household-expenditure basis** since many of these households supplement income with heavy credit use. Moreover, inner-city income often is underreported in official statistics since many residents get their income from the "informal economy" (legal activities such as gardening, childcare, housekeeping, tips, and street vending). The authors suggest a methodology to measure the "retail opportunities" or "retail-sales gaps" by zip code areas, which is demonstrated using a case study for the Denver market. From those retail-sales gap estimates, the authors conclude that "Denver as a whole exports general retail and food items to outside visitors but must shop outside the city for much of its apparel and home needs." The authors recognized, "It could be argued correctly that new retail development in struggling inner city areas is simply a zero-sum game [which means sales are just shifted from one venue to another], with retail sales being redistributed within the same metropolitan area." However, they further asserted, "while sales themselves may simply be redistributed, the multiplied benefits of new economic activity and income combined with lower resource (for example, labor) opportunity costs, are likely to lead to considerably greater social returns for inner city locations."

Reprinted from *ICSC Research Quarterly,* V. 10, No. 4—Winter 2003–04.

- Metro areas and central cities grew the fastest in the south and west
- Suburbs grew faster than cities during the 1990s
- Growth in large cities was fueled by the influx of Asian and Hispanic residents
- Household size is shrinking, but not for Hispanics and Asians
- The 100 largest cities, as a group, became majority minority for the first time in 2000
- The age picture of this country is changing from a pyramid to a pillar as we enter the 20th century
- Minority groups have younger age structures than whites

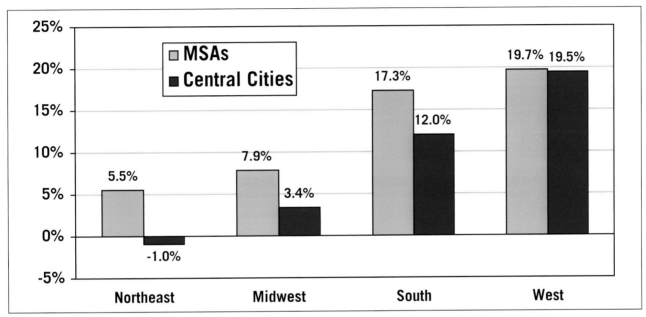

Metro areas and central cities grew the fastest in the south and west

Source: U.S. Census Bureau

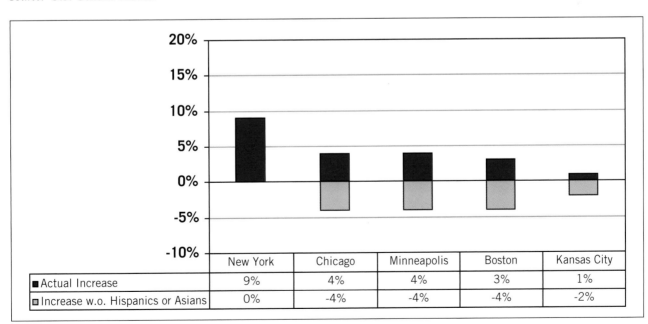

	New York	Chicago	Minneapolis	Boston	Kansas City
■Actual Increase	9%	4%	4%	3%	1%
▨Increase w.o. Hispanics or Asians	0%	-4%	-4%	-4%	-2%

Growth in large cities was fueled by the influx of Asian and Hispanic residents

Source: U.S. Census Bureau

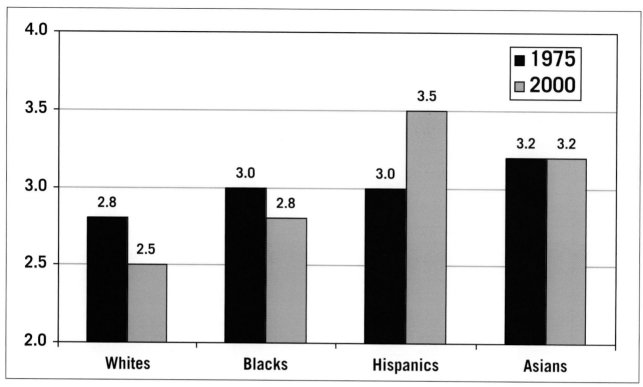

Household size is not shrinking for Hispanics and Asians

Source: U.S. Census Bureau

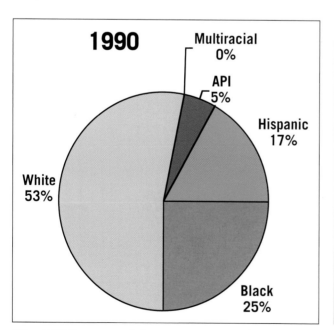 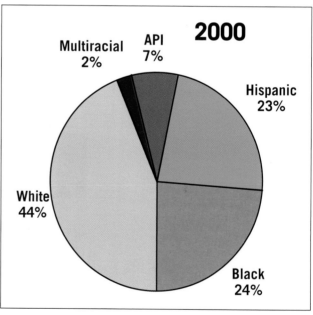

The 100 largest cities, as a group, became majority minority for the first time in 2000

Source: Alan Berube. "Racial Change in the Largest Cities: Evidence from Census 2000." Brookings, Forthcoming

Stony Island Plaza

Stony Island Plaza located in Chicago, Illinois, is an innovative urban community shopping center. Anchored by a Jewel/Osco grocery store, the center contains 177,000 square feet of retail space and is 100% leased.

U.S. Equities Realty, a full-service commercial real estate firm headquartered in Chicago, developed this full-service, high-quality community shopping center in an inner-city, chronically underserved neighborhood. U.S. Equities worked closely with the City of Chicago, the Department of Planning and Development, the local alderman and various community groups to design the center. The city also provided partial project financing through a TIF grant and a Community Development Block Grant (CDBG) loan.

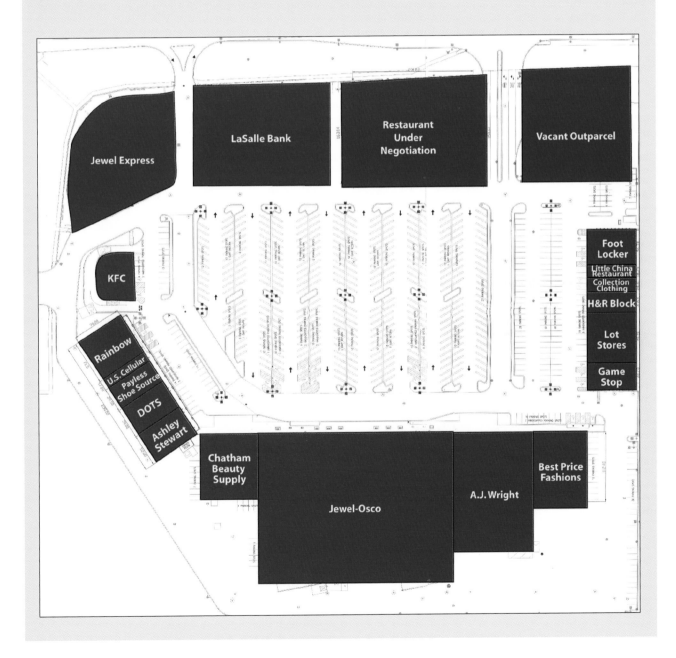

U.S. Equities assembled the land, financed the project by providing equity and obtained private loans as well as city financing. In addition to obtaining the anchor tenant, Jewel/Osco, U.S. Equities convinced several other retailers that despite lower-income demographics, Stony Island Plaza would be an exceptionally successful location. Results have exceeded tenant expectations.

The plaza has parking for 882 vehicles and easy access to major expressways and public transportation. In 2003 U.S. Equities along with the Chicago Transit Authority incorporated a successful bus stop within the plaza.

Stony Island Plaza is a model for inner-city revitalization and proof of the existing untapped markets in underserved urban neighborhoods. Phase I construction was completed in 1999, phase II in 2002 and phase III in 2003.

- **Develop relationships with local real estate professionals**—Local brokers and real estate professionals are familiar with underserved markets and able to identify potential sites and development opportunities.

Retailers

- **Bridge the information gap**—Much of market analysis, such as standard ring analysis, can underestimate these markets. Retailers need to consider the difference in spending habits, purchasing power and population density in urban markets. For example, customers in underserved markets may spend more on apparel (including brand names) than their counterparts in other markets. Companies may need to create "mini-markets" or a smaller focus to better capture market opportunities.
- **Form strategic alliances with other retailers**—Companies who want to enter these markets can be more successful through forming strategic alliances with companies who have experience in underserved markets.
- **Adjust formats**—Some retailers have found that traditional suburban prototype stores are not always successful in urban markets. Retailers should evaluate the creation of smaller prototypes or multistory formats to increase the potential for financial success.
- **Reevaluate the target customer**—With changing demographics in America, retailers may need to reevaluate or expand the profile of their target customer.
- **Consider outside operators**—Many retailers are leaning more heavily on the franchise system as a way to enter underserved markets. In some instances, the new franchisee may not be familiar with urban markets, and retailers may need to offer technical assistance and other types of support to them. Retailers can also develop partnerships with other organizations to help identify franchisees in local communities and offer support through financing packages and training.
- **Develop relationships with local real estate professionals**—Local brokers and real estate professionals are familiar with underserved markets and able to identify potential sites and development opportunities.

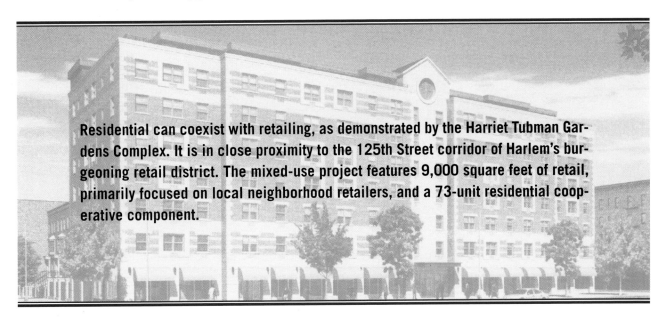

Residential can coexist with retailing, as demonstrated by the Harriet Tubman Gardens Complex. It is in close proximity to the 125th Street corridor of Harlem's burgeoning retail district. The mixed-use project features 9,000 square feet of retail, primarily focused on local neighborhood retailers, and a 73-unit residential cooperative component.

Targeted Marketing and Communication

Retail Chicago is an aggressive outreach program established by Chicago's Mayor Richard M. Daley to work with retailers, brokers and developers and introduce them to the city's underserved but densely populated communities. The program serves as a "One Stop Shop" to address the retail development sector's questions regarding TIF programs, tax incentives, and Enterprise and Empowerment Zone funding, and expedite the retailer's entry into the city. Retail Chicago's goal is accomplished through one-on-one meetings with developers and retailers, which include taking elected city officials to ICSC's annual Spring Convention, where they have prearranged appointments with retailers; maintaining a website with current information on Retail Chicago and Department of Planning and Development programs; and conducting ward tours with the elected officials and representatives of the retail industry to communicate mid- and long-term development goals for each community. Retail Chicago also maintains a current database of active retailers, brokers and developers, has a quarterly newsletter and has ongoing contact with over 120 community agencies in Chicago (Chamber of Commerce, community development corporations, etc.) to help foster and facilitate development opportunities.

Customized Market Data

The Kilduff Company, LLC is a retail real estate development company engaged in providing urban redevelopment projects and development consultation to entities focused on urban revitalization. Since 1997, Kilduff has been engaged in cities across the country, developing projects and assisting municipalities, community-based organizations and faith-based institutions in revitalizing their neighborhoods and retail districts. A critical part of the revitalization process has been the reintroduction of national retailers to the urban marketplace. Perhaps the most important part of this process involves the accurate portrayal of urban market potential to the retail community. The Kilduff Company has formed a partnership with MetroEdge, a market research business of ShoreBank Corporation, to meet this critical objective. MetroEdge recognizes that specialized analysis is needed to identify untapped market opportunities that can spur neighborhood revitalization in an economically viable way. Conventional approaches to retail location analysis and site selection do not work well in the fast-changing, diverse urban marketplace. Specialized data and metrics used by the Kilduff/MetroEdge team in cities such as Indianapolis, San Antonio, Minneapolis, and Chicago include indicators of neighborhood trends using local datasets that are essential for developing new business opportunities. Presenting more accurate market information to the retail and real estate development sectors increases their ability to assess and pursue new urban opportunities.

The overall cost of a project is a key part of the development equation, and in an urban market it's a given that the factors of time and money are usually even bigger. All things being equal, the construction, development and rehabilitation cost is often a major deal-breaker. While many of these challenges are not unique to underserved markets, but are in fact encountered in most urban locations, they can have negative impacts on attracting development to underserved communities. In addition, meeting local government parking requirements is often a challenge in underserved markets because of the cost and the size of available parcels of land.

Many developers that have completed projects in underserved markets concur that one of the primary challenges they face in developing in urban markets is the increased amount of time it takes to formulate the deals due to multiple parcel owners, cumbersome approval and permitting processes and cross-governmental approvals (layers of approval process). These issues can increase the amount of time to complete a project twofold. In development time equates to money, so the increased amount of time increases the cost of the project for the developer and the retailer.

Section Highlights:

- It can take longer and may be more complicated to develop in an urban area, which translates to higher costs. Reducing the time it takes to develop, and therefore the costs, can help promote more development in underserved markets.
- Cost of site preparedness and rehabilitation can be more expensive in these markets.
- While urban markets are generally more pedestrian-friendly, the reality is that people still need cars/parking or access to transportation.

The Renovation of The Century Shopping Centre

Built in 1925, The Century Shopping Centre in Chicago, Illinois, began as "The Diversey Theatre," a 3,000-seat vaudeville and photoplay theatre where live acts and circuses once entertained. Shortly before World War II, Chicago's dominant movie tycoons Balaban and Katz acquired The Diversey. Renaming it The Century, it went on to become one of Chicago's great moviehouses of the North Side, with such names as Greta Garbo, Cary Grant and Clark Gable flickering across the silver screen.

As movie trends changed, large theatres such as The Century became unprofitable. When The Century's lease expired in the early 1970's, it was rumored to be torn down. A local development company acquired the property and transformed The Century into its present structural state: a seven-level unique vertical shopping centre. In addition, they built a seven-level parking garage that houses 500 automobiles. At the time, The Century was known as a small neighborhood shopping center catering to a one-mile radius with a mixture of national chains and local retailers.

Purchased in 1994, the current owners saw the need for a complete redevelopment of the 150,000-sf center. The center housed major tenants such as Bally Total Fitness and a 50,000-sf upscale health club facility, in addition to major retailers such as Victoria's Secret, Bath & Body Works, Express and Tweeter Audio/Video, but the neighborhood was underserved in the areas of new upscale retail, food and entertainment. Beginning in 1998, the entire façade and interior of the center was changed to bring to the center Landmark's Century Centre Cinema: a 7-screen state-of-the-art fine art and independent theater chain, and new retailers such as the Aveda Institute: a beauty care/cosmetics retail store and a 10,000-sf beauty school and Kaplan Educational Center. The shopping center remained open during the two year renovation, adding new carpet, vertical transportation, railings and signage. The center is currently in negotiations to bring a 15,000-sf food emporium to the building in the fall of 2004.

Before: original exterior of The Diversey Theatre, year 1925

After: exterior of building, year 2000

Suggestions to Four Critical Interest Groups

Community

- **Be more flexible on design issues**—Many redevelopment projects include historic preservation issues. Being realistic about the cost and being willing to collaborate with a developer on meeting the historical and aesthetic needs of a neighborhood can mean the difference between the success and failure of a project.

Whittwood Town Center—Whittier, California

Perkowitz + Ruth, along with landscape architects EPT Consulting of San Juan Capistrano, created the Whittwood Town Center design concept, which pays homage to the eclectic Whittier architectural heritage. Located at Whittier Boulevard and Santa Gertrudes Avenue in Whittier City, California, the center, which is a redevelopment of the existing Whittwood Mall, embraces the existing diverse range of styles and is designed to look like it has evolved and matured over time. A multitenant upscale residential district of 150 town homes will be added to complete this village within the city of Whittier, and the project will encompass 792,476 square feet.

Target will join existing anchors JCPenney, Mervyn's, Sears and Vons grocery. Renderings illustrate how Target will reflect the center's architectural vision to avoid anything "themey" or garish and to impart a vibrant and cohesive architectural environment with exciting façades, warm materials and a unifying, rich palette of colors.

- **Add character to the retail project**—Underserved markets often need a fresh and modern approach to attract customers through aesthetical architectural design.
- **Work with local government to identify and market sites**—Working with government officials to identify and market sites will make it easier and quicker for developers to identify sites that are ready for development.
- **Understand the nature of the development process**—When recruiting retail to a previously underserved market it is important for the local community to understand the requirements of successful development, such as the need for retail concentration and co-tenancies. For example, this may mean the need to initially develop much larger parcels of land to bring in a large group of retailers at once.
- **Assist in land assembly**—Community groups and community development corporations can help with the land assembly and participate in the development process.

Government

- **Facilitate site assembling/acquisition**—If retailers or owners won't release leases and/or land, local governments may need to use condemnation rights to move the development process forward. Cities should consider implementing programs that can provide land at a low or reduced cost.

When recruiting retail to a previously underserved market it is important to understand the need for retail concentration and co-tenancies, as the University Village at North Avenue and Cicero in Chicago exemplifies with Marshalls & A.J. Wright. University Village, which opened in 2001, encompasses 16 acres and has a 181,000-s.f. GLA.

The University Village project also includes such national retailers as Old Navy, Cub Foods, The Children's Place, Radio Shack, Rent-A-Center, Dots, Payless Shoes, City Sports, GNC, GameStop, Sketchers, Wendy's, and Pizza Hut.

Metro Development Authority

Louisville is the first city its size in over thirty years to merge city and county governments—becoming the 16th-largest city in the U.S.A. One of the priorities when Mayor Jerry Abramson took office on January 6, 2003, was to enhance neighborhoods with quality retail development.

The mayor established The Retail Development Division (RDD) of the Metro Development Authority (MDA) to create new opportunities. The RDD administers the **COOL** (Corridors Of Opportunity in Louisville) program, which encourages and facilitates retail development along Louisville Metro's commercial corridors to enhance neighborhood quality of life. Though the RDD administers the **COOL** program, it is actually an umbrella initiative of Mayor Abramson's comprising all that every city and outside agency can do collectively to improve quality of life through retail development.

The RDD identifies neighborhood areas underserved by retail business and encourages businesses to locate along the commercial corridors of the area. A high value is placed upon locating retail within existing and underutilized space.

The RDD works with residents, landowners, retailers, developers, real estate professionals, lenders, land use attorneys, government agencies and others to encourage and facilitate retail development. **COOL** functions include site identification, demographic analysis, advocacy within the approvals process, recruiting local and national retail businesses, utilizing incentives, and more. Sometimes **COOL** touches a project in a small way and other times in a large way.

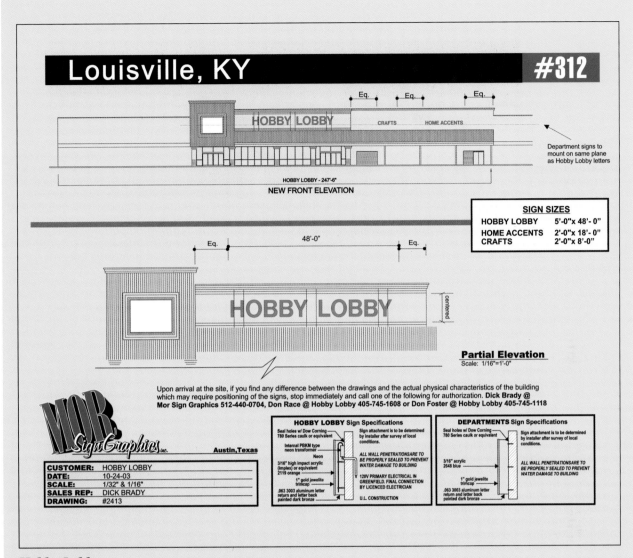

Louisville, KY #312

HOBBY LOBBY CRAFTS HOME ACCENTS

Department signs to mount on same plane as Hobby Lobby letters

Eq. Eq. Eq.

HOBBY LOBBY - 247'-6"
NEW FRONT ELEVATION

SIGN SIZES	
HOBBY LOBBY	5'-0"x 48'- 0"
HOME ACCENTS	2'-0"x 18'- 0"
CRAFTS	2'-0"x 8'-0"

Eq. 48'-0" Eq.

HOBBY LOBBY centered

Partial Elevation
Scale: 1/16"=1'-0"

Upon arrival at the site, if you find any difference between the drawings and the actual physical characteristics of the building which may require positioning of the signs, stop immediately and call one of the following for authorization. **Dick Brady @ Mor Sign Graphics 512-440-0704, Don Race @ Hobby Lobby 405-745-1608 or Don Foster @ Hobby Lobby 405-745-1118**

M.O.R. Sign Graphics inc. Austin, Texas

CUSTOMER:	HOBBY LOBBY
DATE:	10-24-03
SCALE:	1/32" & 1/16"
SALES REP:	DICK BRADY
DRAWING:	#2413

HOBBY LOBBY Sign Specifications

Seal holes w/ Dow Corning 780 Series caulk or equivalent
Internal PBKM type neon transformer
Neon
3/16" high impact acrylic (implex) or equivalent 2119 orange
1" gold jewelite trimcap
.063 3003 aluminum letter return and letter back painted dark bronze

Sign attachment is to be determined by installer after survey of local conditions.
ALL WALL PENETRATIONS ARE TO BE PROPERLY SEALED TO PREVENT WATER DAMAGE TO BUILDING
120V PRIMARY ELECTRICAL IN GREENFIELD. FINAL CONNECTION BY LICENCED ELECTRICIAN
U.L. CONSTRUCTION

DEPARTMENTS Sign Specifications

Seal holes w/ Dow Corning 780 Series caulk or equivalent
3/16" acrylic 2648 blue
1" gold jewelite trimcap
.063 3003 aluminum letter return and letter back painted dark bronze

Sign attachment is to be determined by installer after survey of local conditions.
ALL WALL PENETRATIONS ARE TO BE PROPERLY SEALED TO PREVENT WATER DAMAGE TO BUILDING

Hobby Lobby

The Louisville (Kentucky) Metro Development Authority appealed to Hobby Lobby by identifying a former HQ Hardware site that could be a successful location for Hobby Lobby, which prefers existing big box buildings. Since that time the government agency has assisted with the permitting process, and is assisting in the recruitment of additional retailers for the balance of the building and for a parcel next door. This redeveloped big box opened in February 2004.

Penn Station

Penn Station was already in talks with the landlord when COOL was asked to contribute to this project. Though there were some lease negotiation issues, they were quickly resolved. COOL assisted the project by advocating and arranging assistance from a number of local and state-level agencies. Just previously, the Business Development & Finance division of MDA had redeveloped the streetscape of the area (including brick-accented sidewalks) and executed façade loans with many of the building owners along the street.

This neighborhood, Beechmont, is a middle-class area with the asset of having a parkway and major park nearby, both designed by Frederick Law Olmsted (designer of New York's Central Park). Whereas the neighborhood lacked any sitdown restaurants, Penn Station was the first of several to move into the area.

Gold's Gym

Located in a former Furrow's location, this is the most expansive and finely appointed Gold's Gym in this region of the country. It addressed one of COOL's biggest concerns—empty big boxes.

COOL originally attempted to recruit a Kohl's Department Store to the site, but in the end the promotion of the area in general caught the attention of the Gold's owner.

Staff from COOL are currently evaluating opportunities to improve the streetscape of the area to capitalize on the investment and recruit other retail-oriented redevelopment.

Felice Winery

This retail business and landlord has renovated a vacant Market St. building in the developing Gallery District, but also across the street from Louisville's largest homeless shelter. The building has undergone a major renovation including the addition of arched doorways through exterior brick walls, a patio, and a large wine cellar and processing facility. Though Felice is the largest tenant, the building will also house a pottery artist gallery, a restaurant, and other retail and office space.

COOL offered public financing and recruited additional retail tenants. Currently, COOL is identifying sites for an urban vineyard from which Felice Winery will grow its own grapes nearby.

- **Identify and market sites**—In order to reduce the amount of time for a developer, and therefore the overall cost, governments should help identify and market sites that are ready for development.
- **Market financial incentives**—Local governments should make retailers and developers aware of tax credits and other financial incentives that will help offset the cost of development in these markets.
- **Streamline and expedite the application process**—Cities should streamline their application processes. The time schedule to take advantage of tax incentives is too long and the process is too cumbersome; developers cannot hold properties for the time required for the entire process of necessary reviews and approvals to be completed. There is a perception by the development community that many of these programs are too cumbersome and time-consuming, and are, therefore, not used to offset development costs when evaluating new locations.

Linden, Ohio

BACKGROUND

The Linden community of Columbus, Ohio, was first settled in the late 1700s as part of a federal land grant to reward veterans' military service during the Revolutionary War. By the late 19th century, the community had transitioned from a loose confederation of farms to an independent municipality with a prosperous commercial corridor and strong residential base. The community was annexed into the city of Columbus in 1913 and continued a strong, prosperous period of growth until the end of World War II.

Like so many other American neighborhoods, the construction of the interstate highway system, population deconcentration and suburbanization had adverse effects on Linden. In recent years, significant attention has been paid to the revitalization of the housing stock and the commercial corridor of the community. The Greater Linden Development Corporation (GDLC), the neighborhood's community development corporation, was created in 1994 to help address some of these issues. They have been integral in implementing a series of strategic efforts to help enhance the attractiveness of the marketplace.

GREATER LINDEN BUSINESS NETWORK

GLDC created the Greater Linden Business Network (GLBN) to help strengthen and enhance the local business community. Ideally, if the establishments that already exist in the neighborhood can become more successful, it will validate the community regionally as a good place to locate and/or conduct business. GLBN's monthly meetings allow business leaders to network with their peers while learning about timely topics such as increasing security at your company, writing a business plan and getting a loan. GLBN also gives its members tangible returns on their investment by:

- Having the opportunity to place a business profile in *The Greater Linden News* at no charge. This publication has a circulation of over 12,000 and can raise a business's profile in the community
- Using the Welcome Wagon program to promote your business to new Linden residents.
- Enjoy discounts from participating GLBN members or promote your company by offering a member-to-member discount.
- Receive scholarships or partial scholarships for educational seminars (as funds permit).
- Get discounts on advertising in *The Greater Linden News* and the business directory.

TECHNICAL ASSISTANCE

While GLDC does not offer direct technical assistance to individuals interested in starting or expanding a business, they provide connectivity between the community and the vast series of resources that exist at the federal, state and local level. They also utilize their unique knowledge of the neighborhood to attempt to broker deals between tenants, landlords and entities interested in investing in the community. In this way, GLDC has a good sense of what is occurring in the business community from a grass-roots level.

DESIGN STANDARDS

The Greater Linden Development Corporation has been integral in ensuring that the commercial revitalization projects taking place in the community adhere to traditional urban design standards. A special zoning overlay was adopted by the City Council to mandate that buildings are built with a zero setback, brick façades are maintained or constructed and buildings are constructed at a scale appropriate to the style and density of similar commercial corridors and that parking requirements reflect the reality of an urban setting.

NEIGHBORHOOD IDENTIFICATION

The Linden neighborhood engaged in several strategies to brand their commercial revitalization areas and create a cohesive sense of place. Identification signage was designed and placed at key entrance points in a commercial node. This signage featured the words "Welcome to Linden" and included a graphic of the GLDC's logo. This logo has been in use since the CDC's creation and has come to symbolize the neighborhood.

At key commercial revitalization nodes, the standard cobra-head streetlights that are often found in business districts have been replaced by pedestrian-scaled lighting. These lights help pedestrian consumers feel like an active participant in the urban environment rather than an afterthought, awash in the indiscriminant incandescent light. These lights are also of a higher quality than the standard cobra head, are easier to maintain, and do a better job of illuminating the commercial building stock at night. The lightposts also feature mast arms where 18″ × 36″ banners

Carryout

can be displayed. These banners are a mixture of Greater Linden's logo, the name of the neighborhood and a seasonal message that is rotated throughout the year.

Restaurant/offices

- **Revise code requirements**—Often codes and ordinances are in place that hinder the redevelopment process and do not support mixed-use development or creative use of limited urban space.
- **Recognize the importance of parking**—Cities need to acknowledge the importance of parking and modify existing codes or implement new ones that recognize that many urban residents will use cars to shop and provide for creative ways to meet parking standards.
- **Evaluate condition of Brownfield sites**—By conducting Phase 1 and Phase 2 assessments of Brownfield sites, local governments can determine the extent of contamination and provide more certainty in assessing environmental issues and remediation costs, and this can help developers better evaluate the cost of development.
- **Publicly fund infrastructure improvements**—Local governments can help offset development costs and can leverage a number of funding mechanisms, including tax increment financing to finance infrastructure and public works improvements.

Developers

- **Fully investigate available incentives**—Developers should fully explore tax and financial incentives available in underserved markets before deciding the project is too expensive.
- **Actively promote urban/underserved market expertise to retailers**—Developers should aggressively promote opportunities to retailers. Many retailers indicate that they are interested in relocating in underserved markets, but they have difficulty finding experienced local urban developers. Developers may find more tenants by filling this need.
- **Pass through incentives to retailers**—Retailers also experience increased costs locating in urban markets. Developers might find ways to pass through financial offsets to tenants through increased tenant allowances.
- **Lower rents initially**—To attract retailers and help offset their increased costs, offer lower rents during the initial development of the center and increase the rents as the retailers' sales performance increases.

Retailers

- **Fully investigate available incentives**—Retailers acting as developers should fully explore tax and financial incentives available in underserved markets before deciding the project is too expensive.
- **Adapt store configurations and be a more flexible tenant**—Retailers should recognize that land is at a premium in urban markets, and consequently there may be less square footage to meet standard store configurations. They should provide alternative urban configurations and inform developers and brokers of alternative requirements to aid in site selection and development. These smaller store prototypes or smaller footprints will also reduce cost of development and rent.

Joint financing spreads the risks among financial institutions in new projects in underserved markets. Such was the case at West Cliff Shopping Plaza in Dallas, Texas, where lenders included Chase Bank of Texas, Bank United, Northern Trust Bank, The Retail Initiative, and Bank of Texas.

A well-stocked deli at Albertson's supermarket in West Cliff Shopping Plaza puts forth its best image to new customers.

Urban America's Eastover Shopping Center

Founded in 1998 to become America's preeminent vehicle for fiscally and socially prudent investment in inner-city commercial real estate, UrbanAmerica (UA) owns and operates a $324 million portfolio of 28 properties. UrbanAmerica funnels institutional dollars into previously neglected investment opportunities and creates jobs by employing local vendors to service its properties.

Eastover Shopping Center, with 249,000 square feet of retail property and located in Oxon Hill, Maryland, which has a low-to-moderate-income census tract, was purchased in March 2000 and through sound leasing and management efforts has achieved 20% total NOI growth at the property since acquisition.

New tenants brought to Eastover through an aggressive lease-up campaign include Shoe Express, Fashion Cents, Ablaze, Personnel Plus, Eddie's Outlet, Burger King, and Shoe Stop.

UrbanAmerica is not solely interested in filling vacancies but has also made successful investments in safety at their properties. At Eastover, UA helped to finance the construction of a new 22,000-sf police station located on the grounds of the center, thereby fulfilling an objective to improve the communities in which they invest.

Genesis LA

More than a decade after the civil unrest that shook the city, the South Los Angeles community surrounding the Vermont/Slauson intersection finally has a new full-service market. The new supermarket, Gigante, was built on four acres owned and developed by the Vermont Slauson Economic Development Corporation, a seasoned nonprofit dedicated to the economic revitalization of the community around the intersection of Vermont and Slauson avenues. In addition to the 50,000-square-foot Gigante store, VSEDC also developed a 5,000-square-foot pad for Burger King, another 4,000-square-foot office building to serve as their new headquarters and 230 parking spaces. The development is expected to produce 170 new jobs. Financing came from several sources, including the Los Angeles Community Development Bank, the Office of

From left to right, Los Angeles Mayor James K. Hahn, Kelli Bernard—Vice President of Real Estate for Genesis LA Economic Growth Corp., LA City Councilwoman Jan Perry, Brad Rosenberg—CEO and President of Genesis, and Marva Smith Battle-Bey—Executive Director of Vermont Slauson Economic Development Corporation.

the Mayor, the U.S. Department of Commerce, the U.S. Department of Health & Human Services, private lenders and Genesis LA Economic Growth Corporation. As with most projects in the older built-out communities of Los Angeles, the amount of funding available for a project does not cover the amount required to complete the development. It is for this reason that Genesis LA created a family of funds that provide loans to cover these gaps. In this case, Genesis LA used a small fund created with the express purpose of providing gap financing for urban infill development in Los Angeles. This fund allows Genesis to act as an equity investor with low-cost funds that are repaid by the project's takeout permanent financing.

Customize Market Analysis

Chesterfield Square is South Los Angeles's largest commercial project in more than a decade. Developed by Katell Properties, the 285,00-square-foot, $50 million shopping center's official grand opening took place in April 2002, to coincide with the tenth anniversary of the Los Angeles-area riots. The Square features tenants such as Home Depot, Food 4 Less, McDonald's, Radio Shack, IHOP, and Starbucks. Open since July 2001, Home Depot spokesman Chuck Sifuentes says the store is operating 10% ahead of the $50 million in sales projected for the first year. Food 4 Less says its Chesterfield Square opening was the best ever for the chain. Prior to the development of Chesterfield Square, there were 1.1 million residents living within a 5-mile radius with almost no mainstream retailers present. A study by Pepperdine University found that while median household income was $12,000 less than the national median, local residents were spending $900 million a year outside of South Central.

Underserved Market Expertise—Johnson Development Corporation

Urban Real Estate Fund Redevelops Mall in Milwaukee as First Investment

Adapted from an article by Elisabeth Pena

The 55-acre Capitol Court Shopping Mall in Milwaukee, WI, is being redeveloped as the first investment of the national urban real estate fund Canyon-Johnson Urban Fund LP. The $300 million fund plans to redevelop the mall through a partnership with Boulder Venture of Milwaukee. The $53 million project, which will be renamed Midtown Center,

will include the demolition of the existing mall, followed by the construction of about 606,000 sq. ft. of retail space anchored by a 150,000-sq.-ft. Wal-Mart. The center also will include national credit retailers, entertainment components and restaurants. Construction at the center began in September and Wal-Mart is slated to open in May.

The Milwaukee investment is inline with the fund's investment strategy, which is to identify, enhance and capture value through the acquisition, development and redevelopment of urban real estate and the origination of mortgages secured by urban real estate. Owned by Canyon Capital Realty Advisors LLC, a money management firm, and Johnson Development Corp., the closed-end real estate fund expects to provide for and foster economic opportunities for underserved urban neighborhoods.

The Midtown Center project epitomizes the opportunities available in urban America say executives at the Canyon-Johnson Urban Fund. The Midtown Center marketplace has a large population with spending power and lacks service and amenities.

Executives in charge of the deal say the fund was created to capitalize on existing opportunities and fill existing demand, not to create demand; it is not a regentrification, but a revitalization of an existing community. The fund plans to seek joint ventures with local owner operators, as well as opportunities that could be provided through the joint ventures of the Johnson Development.

Magic Johnson Theaters / Johnson Development Corporation (JDC) is opening first-run movie theaters in inner-city neighborhoods and establishing successful joint ventures to bring other retail services to these areas. JDC partnered with Sony Retail Entertainment to develop theaters in Los Angeles, Atlanta, and Houston and has plans to open additional theaters. The first theater was constructed in a South Central Los Angeles retail mall and is among the top-grossing theaters in the nation. Since the theater's opening, occupancy rates in the mall increased from 60 percent to 98 percent, and other mall tenants report increases in sales. JDC

Founded by Earvin "Magic" Johnson in 1993, Johnson Development works to provide a business stimulus fostering local economic growth and creating financial empowerment in neglected minority urban and suburban neighborhoods. The company develops movie theaters, restaurants and coffee shops and is involved in 50/50 joint ventures with Starbucks Coffee, T.G.I. Friday's Restaurants and Magic Johnson Theaters. The fund's managers say they are taking a close look at all the tenancy options that Johnson Development is involved in. The fund is in the early stages of discussions to fill other spaces at the Midtown Center.

has entered into other joint ventures with 24 Hour Fitness, Starbucks, and TGI Fridays to open multiple stores. The theaters alone have created more than 350 jobs, and JDC does much of its contracting with local minority-owned suppliers.

In 1998, Starbucks Coffee Company and Earvin "Magic" Johnson's company, Johnson Development Corporation (JDC), formed Urban Coffee Opportunities, LLC (UCO) to enhance the development of Starbucks retail stores in ethnically diverse urban and suburban neighborhoods across the country. Starbucks and JDC both recognized that there was a segment of the market that could support further economic development of major high-end retailers. As a result, the two companies began discussions on how they could work together to open Starbucks locations in these communities. The 50/50 joint venture combines the retail strength of Starbucks with JDC's knowledge of real estate in key metropolitan markets and relationships in local communities.

At the start of 2004, there were 57 UCO stores in locations including Los Angeles, New York, Seattle, Chicago, Detroit, Atlanta, San Diego and Washington, D.C. The stores have been embraced by community members and have provided local jobs as well as employment opportunities for qualified minority contractors and service vendors.

Community involvement is important to the partners (employees) of the UCO stores, as exhibited through the efforts of a UCO store in Florida that is located on a main corridor that runs through Miami. Other retail stores and restaurants are planning renovations to locations along

this portion of Biscayne Boulevard. The UCO store is currently working to support Safespace, an organization committed to the prevention of domestic violence in the Miami area. The store provided a donation to Safespace at its grand opening celebration. In addition, the store regularly provides a donation of pastries and coffee to Safespace and is determining additional opportunities to provide support throughout the year.

Operating costs tend to be higher in urban markets, however, potential sales could far exceed higher operating costs because of higher concentrations of population, reduced competition, and greater sales potential.

Retailers find that recruitment and retention and shrinkage are significant challenges faced in underserved markets. There are several ways to address these operational issues. Establishing urban markets as a positive opportunity for employee growth and development can help recruit and retain the most qualified personnel. This in turn can help address the strong customer service element that must be present when meeting the needs of the inner-city underserved markets. Inner-city consumers expect the friendly and knowledgeable salespeople, in-stock merchandise and speedy checkout lanes found at many suburban locations. Positive employment experiences also help influence employee loyalty and turnover at inner-city locations. Improved loyalty and lower turnover help lower shrinkage and overall operating expenditures through savings in recruitment and training costs.

Community approval and support of new development plays a tremendous role in the success of development in underserved markets. It is critical to develop partnerships with local community organizations, employ local residents, and become an integral part of the local community culture as a normal course of operations.

Section Highlights:

- Operating costs are often higher in urban, underserved markets.
- Higher operating costs can be offset by higher sales potential of these markets.
- Accessibility to public transportation and improved safety and security can help recruit and retain employees.
- Government tax incentive programs can assist in reduction of operating costs.

Suggestions to Four Critical Interest Groups

Community

- **Help address retailers' hiring needs**—Communities need to connect retailers to pools of qualified applicants through community organizations and neighborhood churches. Work with local government to promote the importance of hiring locally and the importance of training staff in the skill sets needed to operate effectively within underserved markets.

City of Chicago Mayor's Office of Workforce Development and TIFWorks

The City of Chicago Mayor's Office of Workforce Development (MOWD) administers *TIFWorks,* a city program that helps companies in qualified Tax Increment Financing (TIF) districts pay for various job-training activities.

"TIFWorks is invaluable for companies that want to upgrade or expand the skills of their workforce," explained MOWD Commissioner Jackie Edens. "It's especially useful to pay for the training of new workers."

Businesses located within eligible TIF districts can use TIFWorks funds for workforce development activities such as customer service skills training, English-as-a-Second-Language instruction, and industry-specific job training.

Applicants located within or expanding into a TIF can be individual employers; multiple companies with any type of common training needs; and organizations such as industrial councils, community development corporations, and business or trade groups that agree to train and place workers in TIF-located businesses.

To date, 21 TIFWorks applications have been approved for funding across the city for a total of $1.35 million. Seven companies are currently engaged in training.

TIFWorks operates in cooperation with the City's Department of Planning and Development, the Department of Finance and the Chicago Workforce Board.

Tax Increment Financing allows the city to invest public money to improve a particular area for commercial or industrial development. This public investment is later repaid through the future property tax revenue, or increment, generated by companies that locate in the area.

TIFWORKS IN ACTION: THE AVANZA SUPERMARKET PROJECT

Avanza Supermarket, located at 5220 S. Pulaski in the 63rd and Pulaski Tax Increment Finance district, has been awarded $150,000 of TIF funds to conduct an on-the-job training program for 200 new and current employees.

Through TIFWorks, the Avanza employees will be trained on a variety of workplace topics, such as:

- Food safety and produce identification
- Register training
- Customer service
- Powered industrial truck certification
- Supervisory and management
- Shipping and receiving
- Computer skills

The TIFWorks grant offsets the costs of training their workers with the aim of making Avanza more competitive in the supermarket industry, as well as giving their employees valuable skills to make them more competitive in their current and future jobs.

OSCO PHARMACY TECHNICIAN TRAINING

MOWD has also partnered with Boys and Girls Club of Chicago and Osco Drug to help young Chicagoans prepare for Pharmacy Technician jobs.

Beginning in early 2003, in-school and out-of-school youth (aged 16 and up) enrolled in Boys and Girls Club programs throughout the city were selected to participate in a Pre-Pharmacy Technician training program based on aptitude, academic performance, and interest in pharmaceutics. Selected participants were interviewed and assessed by Osco and recommended for training.

The first half of the eight-week training was conducted on-site at Boys and Girls Club's 2102 W. Monroe St location, where participants learned topics such as the role of a pharmacy technician, drug coding and classifications, and pharmacy terminology. Trainees were then required to pass a 4-hour computer tutorial and complete 36 hours of training and a 2-week internship at Osco. Upon successful completion of the training and internship, participants were tested for state licensing. The cost of state license testing and training ($40 and approximately $600, respectively, per participant) is paid for by MOWD.

(From L-R): Fannieleah Brown (Boys & Girls Club of Chicago [BGCC]), Sharon Simmons (BGCC), Maiya Dodson (Program Graduate), Anthony Jones (Osco Division Pharmacy Manager), Karla M. Nunnally (Osco Pharmacy Manager), Lorraine Norsworthy (BGCC)

Of the project's four initial participants, all completed training and received a state license. Osco hired two project participants for pharmacy technician jobs with an hourly wage of $8.65. Recruitment for a second class of up to twelve students is already under way, with training expected to commence in January 2004.

The Pharmacy Technician training responds to the growing demand for pharmacists—according to the Bureau of Labor Statistics, employment opportunities for pharmacists are expected to grow faster than the average through the year 2010 due largely to the increased pharmaceutical needs of a larger and older population and greater use of medication.

MOWD, NATIONAL RETAIL FEDERATION, AND CVS PHARMACY

The National Retail Federation (NRF) has initiated a program to offer skill development opportunities in the customer service area. Once skills are obtained, NRF is piloting a process by which those skills are recognized and certified. This customer service certification program enables those who pass to demonstrate to current and future employers that they possess customer service abilities. This certification, while developed for the retail sector, can apply in virtually any sector. This nationally recognized certification, once implemented, will provide both training and certification on-line.

The National Retail Federation identified the necessary competencies, developed the certification process and is marketing the initiative to the business community. CVS Pharmacy is among the first businesses to adopt the certification as a valuable employee screening tool. As evidence, CVS has agreed to extend an interview to candidates who are successful in obtaining the certification. With new CVS stores opening in Chicago, CVS representatives will use the NRF Customer Service certification to streamline their employee selection process.

As the administrative entity of the local workforce investment system, the Mayor's Office of Workforce Development (MOWD) has plans to deliver the NRF training and certification through its network of One-Stop Career Centers and Affiliate centers.

Together, NRF, CVS and MOWD will implement the certification program throughout Chicago to more effectively address this crucial skill shortage area.

Government

- **Streamline occupancy permitting and approval processes**—Acquiring a letter of occupancy can be a time-consuming process that adds to operating cost. Cities can assign an ombudsman or have someone responsible for shepherding this process for the retailers. Cities in general can help lower overall cost by reducing the time required for the permitting and approval processes.
- **Develop tax credits and abatements**—In addition to lowering development costs, local governments might consider putting together tax credit and abatement packages that

can be utilized by retailers to offset their operating costs. This could include employee tax credits, energy credits, and reductions in recycling and trash removal fees.

- **Apply local job training and recruiting resources to retail jobs**—Currently, many cities do not apply their workforce development and recruiting resources to retail industry jobs. Access to these resources can add value for retailers and positively impact their operating costs. There are well-developed career ladders in the retail industry and applying job training resources to this industry would expand opportunities for potential employees in the community.
- **Help generate sales and improve commercial viability of community**—Co-locating government offices in targeted underserved markets can serve to increase foot traffic and help generate sales for local businesses, which help offset higher operations cost of these markets. Municipalities should consider creating business incubators for local businesses to help improve commercial viability of the area and create opportunities for local entrepreneurs. Actively support and assist in the improvement of retail that is already located in the community, which will support recruitment efforts of new retail.
- **Help develop local franchise operators**—Develop strategies to offset operation costs and provide financing packages for local entrepreneurs who may be successful franchisees but lack capital. These local franchisees can facilitate retail attraction and create a balance between national and local retail development.
- **Assist with marketing and advertising**—Local communities can offset advertising costs of retailers by marketing and promoting communities and developments, or supplement the existing advertising costs of the retailer.

Developers

- **Consider safety and security in design**—Promoting safety and a sense of security for customers and employees is important to the success of store operations and employee recruitment and retention.
- **Emphasize public transportation**—Incorporating access to public transportation into developments will help retailers attract customers as well as recruit and retain employees.

Retailers

- **Develop a comprehensive market entry strategy**—Retailers should bring neighborhood groups into the process and develop a plan for becoming a viable part of the community. This will have a positive impact on employees and customer loyalty, which will serve to reduce both internal and external shrinkage and create positive relationships between new businesses and the community.
- **Focus on customer service**—Excellent and attentive customer service is critical to the success of new and existing business in underserved markets.
- **Educate internal stakeholders about market potential**—The increased cost of operations in underserved markets can be offset by the potential sales results. Inner-city

density is what ultimately drives its market potential, as the higher population of residents per square mile in the inner city creates its greater spending power and balances out its lower per capita incomes.

Washington, DC Marketing Center

The Washington, DC Marketing Center is a 501(c)(3) nonprofit organization with a mission of facilitating economic development in the District of Columbia. As a public private partnership between the District Government and private businesses, a key component of that mission is the attraction of retail to the District. The Center's involvement in ICSC provides an excellent platform in support of this goal, and the Center coordinates the District's ICSC retail outreach effort. New retail stores enhance the District's sales and property tax base, create jobs for DC residents, and allow residents to shop for basic goods and services in the city.

The Center's ICSC outreach is a year-round effort that involves District officials, brokers, commercial developers, and law firms with a real estate emphasis.

The Center also publishes research, economic development trends, and marketing materials to promote the District's retail opportunities, neighborhood demographic profiles, and development dynamic. These printed and electronic presentations are valuable summaries on available sites, incentives, and information retailers seek to make location decisions.

The Center has also partnered with the DC Government and Social Compact to conduct original research on the spending power of "intown" residential markets. The research focused on two District neighborhood clusters and discovered numerous positive trends in population growth, the size of local cash economies, and consumer purchasing power. The findings were published and have been used as a powerful marketing piece for attracting retailers and commercial developers to the District's urban neighborhoods.

The Center participates in at least three ICSC conferences each year. The major meeting in Las Vegas provides the greatest opportunity for interface with retailers, as the Center and its partners host a reception for over 400 attendees, the mayor and DC Council members attend meetings, and two separate dinner events provide opportunities for networking with retailers and developers.

- **Implement comprehensive security measures**—It is important to create a safety and security mind-set from day one that emphasizes the importance of shrinkage reduction. Discussion participants felt shrinkage was best addressed by installation of tight financial and inventory controls and having local management that is attuned to their market area. Visible security that is nonthreatening to customers, and still appropriate for protection of merchandise, is also important to success.
- **Emphasize training and development**—Retailers should maintain focus on the importance and need to have an effective and well-trained management staff, one that reflects a working knowledge of urban markets. It is also important to emphasize the importance of the unique skill sets managers need to operate effectively within underserved markets (e.g. customer service, effective communication style, strong community involvement, commitment to hiring locally, and assessment and evaluation of shrinkage reduction programs). Many retailers find that hiring locally and promoting from within helps develop a management staff with an understanding of urban markets.
- **Consider nontraditional hiring sources**—Retailers should utilize local churches and local faith-based organizations to identify and recruit potential candidates. This can help offset recruitment costs, while developing stronger partnerships with the local community.

Recruitment Partnerships

The Home Depot recently announced plans to partner with the U.S. Department of Labor and its National Business Partnership, a program providing services to unemployed or dislocated workers seeking jobs. The Department of Labor will recruit, screen and refer applicants preparing to join Home Depot. In addition, Home Depot will test a long-term strategy of working with state and local workforce boards in selected markets providing future opportunities to unemployed workers.

Gaining Community Support

Starbucks has several stores that are aligned with specific causes or charitable partners. Since 1995, the company's Rainier Avenue store in Seattle has contributed $50,000 annually to the Zion Preparatory Academy, a private elementary and secondary school primarily serving the African-American community in Seattle. The contributions are primarily funded through the Rainier Avenue store's profits.

Pathmark's Urban Initiative

Pathmark Stores, Inc. is committed to operating in both urban and suburban locations in the New York-New Jersey and Philadelphia metropolitan areas. Approximately a quarter of Pathmark's 143 supermarkets are located in urban communities. Pathmark's industry-leading practice of running safe and clean stores is followed at every location it operates. Similarly, Pathmark's policy of hiring store associates from within each store's trade area gives Pathmark's stores a local, customer-friendly look and excellent customer service.

Pathmark's commitment to urban communities began in the mid-1960s with stores in the Bronx and Camden, New Jersey. Those stores have been modernized numerous times, and are still in operation today. Subsequently, more new stores were opened in urban communities so that today nearly 40 Pathmarks operate in such areas. In 1990, Pathmark formed a joint venture with New Community Corporation, a local nonprofit Community Development Center (CDC), for the development of a Pathmark in Newark. In 1999, in conjunction with The Retail Initiative of Local Initiatives Support Corporation (LISC), a national economic development intermediary, and EHAT, a local nonprofit CDC comprised of the Abyssinian Development Corporation and the East Harlem Triangle, Pathmark opened a new, modern store on 125th Street in Harlem. In 2004, Pathmark will open another store with a local CDC—this one will be another Bronx store with the Mid Bronx Desperadoes group (MBD) located near Crotona Park.

Pathmark's urban stores provide quality products, good values, jobs to local residents and a source of community pride to the communities these stores serve. In the Harlem store, some 275 jobs were created, over 85% of which are filled by local community residents.

50,000-sq.-ft. Harlem Pathmark project at 125th St. & Lexington Ave., New York, NY. Equity investor—The Retail Initiative, Inc.

Survey Results—Importance of Factors Influencing Retailers' Decision to Establish Stores in Underserved Markets

Factor	Very Significant	Somewhat Significant	Total Columns 2 and 3	Not Important	No. of Responses
1. Insufficient concentration of your target customer	72%	16%	**88%**	13%	96
2. Length of time to complete a project	9%	40%	**49%**	51%	95
3. Lack of consumer purchasing power for your product(s)	60%	26%	**86%**	14%	97
4. Inadequate neighborhood infrastructure (e.g., transportation, utilities)	29%	46%	**74%**	26%	94
5. Burdensome taxes relative to other store locations	27%	38%	**65%**	35%	94
6. Real estate costs:			**0%**		
a. Direct purchase price	43%	22%	**64%**	36%	87
b. Construction and development costs	50%	31%	**81%**	19%	88
c. Demolition costs	31%	40%	**72%**	28%	89
d. Environmental remediation	52%	22%	**74%**	26%	90
e. Buildout/Rehabilitation costs	53%	30%	**84%**	16%	92
f. Rent (if not owning property directly)	55%	29%	**85%**	15%	92
7. Site identification	62%	22%	**84%**	16%	94
8. Parcel sizes	41%	33%	**74%**	26%	93
9. Inadequate parking	57%	26%	**83%**	17%	95
10. Lack of amenities to attract out-of-neighborhood employees	46%	35%	**81%**	19%	95
11. Lack of experienced underserved-market developers	28%	34%	**62%**	38%	92
12. Inadequate local labor supply			**0%**		
a. Quantity of labor	38%	32%	**70%**	30%	94
b. Skill level of labor	38%	37%	**74%**	26%	93
13. Crime/Perceived crime	69%	24%	**93%**	7%	96
14. Potential shrinkage	62%	24%	**86%**	14%	95
15. Identifying and forming relationships with key political/community players	13%	47%	**60%**	40%	94
16. Local government resistance to use of eminent domain	14%	26%	**40%**	60%	92
17. Zoning issues	30%	30%	**59%**	41%	91
18. Permitting process	34%	41%	**75%**	25%	93
19. Historic preservation issues	21%	38%	**59%**	41%	92
20. Serving unfamiliar customer base	33%	30%	**63%**	37%	93
21. Community resistance	33%	24%	**58%**	42%	90
22. Market data/Analysis			**0%**		
a. Inaccuracy of available market data	26%	36%	**62%**	38%	92
b. Lack of specialized metrics/models for these markets	20%	40%	**60%**	40%	92
23. Reluctant to be first entrant in the market	24%	29%	**53%**	47%	94
24. Internal company resistance	25%	38%	**63%**	37%	92
25. Higher operating costs	49%	32%	**82%**	18%	93

RESOURCES

This publication is not intended to be a comprehensive document on the subject of why some urban markets remain underserved; instead, it is our hope that this is the next step in a journey to bring much-needed retail services to the citizens of America's underserved urban markets. It will be incumbent upon all stakeholders from the local community, local governments, developers, retailers, and various interest groups to work together in developing strategies and partnerships to meet the needs of these markets.

ICSC and **BSR** are committed to exploring further vehicles through research, publications, and compilation of case studies as well as educational sessions and meetings to facilitate this effort. For more information or a list of related publications and organizations, please contact:

International Council of Shopping Centers
Local Government Relations
1033 N. Fairfax, Suite 404
Alexandria, VA 22314
Phone: 703/549-7404
E-mail: govrel@icsc.org
www.icsc.org

Business for Social Responsibility
Community Investment
609 Mission Street, 2nd Floor
San Francisco, CA 94105
Phone: 415/537-0888
E-mail: info@bsr.org
www.bsr.org

ACKNOWLEDGMENTS

The International Council of Shopping Centers would like to thank the following contributors who offered their time, commitment, and expertise to the production of this publication. Special recognition is due to the International Council of Shopping Center's Alliance and Local Outreach Task Force, which is committed to fostering better relationships between the public and private sector and promoting quality retail development in local communities across America.

Aubrey Avery, Jr.
Consultant
Avery & Associates

Carrie L. Berman
Marketing Manager
U.S. Equities Realty, LLC

Kelli Bernard
Vice President, Real Estate
Genesis L.A. Economic Growth Corp.

Beverly Berry
Director of Retention
City of Detroit

Christopher Berry
Senior Advisor, R&D
MetroEdge

Avis E. Black
Area Real Estate Manager
Safeway Inc.

G. Lamont Blackstone
Principal
G.L. Blackstone & Associates

Alton R. Brown, III, SCSM, CLS
President
The Pelican Group

Archie E. Dishman, CLS
Vice President, Real Estate &
  Construction
One Price Clothing Stores, Inc.

Norris R. Eber, SCSM, CLS
Executive Vice President
Joseph Freed and Associates, LLC

Stanley L. Eichelbaum, SCMD
President
Marketing Developments, Inc.

John Fischer
Assistant Director
Metro Development Authority

Kemper Freeman, Jr.
President
Bellevue Square Managers

John L. Glatz
Chief Operating Officer
JPA Real Estate

Harvey M. Gutman
Senior Vice President,
  Retail Development
Pathmark Stores, Inc.

Jennifer P. Haffey
Real Estate Representative
Starbucks Coffee Company

Sean Hardin
Director of Workforce Solutions, Mayor's
  Office of Workforce Development
City of Chicago

Shelly Herman
President
MetroEdge

Brian Higgins
Program Officer, Community Development
  Collaborative of Greater Columbus
The Enterprise Foundation

Alan J. Hochman
Director of Real Estate
Gap, Inc.

Robert Howard
Senior Consultant, Retail Sector
MetroEdge

Brad M. Hutensky
President
The Hutensky Group

Joseph J. James
Chief Operating Officer
South Carolina Department
of Commerce

Burney Johnson
Director of Planning Activities
City of Detroit

Geoff Kerth
Development Coordinator
The Harlem Irving Companies, Inc.

Lawrence E. Kilduff
President
The Kilduff Company

George Kolb
Administrator
Augusta, GA

Cynthia J. Kratchman
Vice President, Commercial
Retail Division
Insite Commercial Group, LLC

Elizabeth Libby
Communications Director, Mayor's
Office of Workforce Development
City of Chicago

James E. Maurin
Chairman & CEO
Stirling Properties

Richmond S. McCoy
President & CEO
UrbanAmerica, L.P.

Gary D. Rappaport, SCMD,
SCSM, CLS
President
The Rappaport Companies

Randall Roth
Principal
The Endeavor Company

Kelly L. H. Sheppard
Public Relations Manager
Starbucks Coffee Company

William A. Shiel, CLS
Senior Vice President
Walgreen Company

Meredith L. Sisk
Manager of Marketing and
Communications
UrbanAmerica, L.P.

Frances Spencer, SCSM, SCMD
Assistant Commissioner, City of Chicago
Department of Planning & Development

Bral Spight
Principal
SIVIC, LLC

Lori Stein
Property Manager/Marketing Director
NAI Hiffman Asset Management, LLC

Frederick J. Stemmler
President
Manchester Investment Group

Michael G. Stevens, AICP
President
Washington, DC Marketing Center

Lily Tafel
Designer
Perkowitz & Ruth Architects

Dominic Wiker
Director
Baltimore Main Streets